W9-DJM-165

This little book is dedicated to

____

San Diego, California
U.S.A.

ISBN 0-7416-1146-5

www.havocpub.com

Made in China

to be as kind
as a Teddy Bear

LIFT ONE'S
SPIRIT

Because of you my
Spirit soars!

Flowers Tree & Sunshine and Honey Bees
Honey

Because of you, dear angel,
My life has new meaning.

Life surprises us

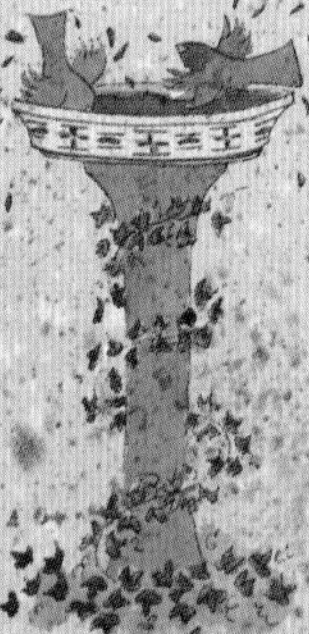

With pleasures great and small,

and you are the angel of
unexpected joy!
God Loves Us
Big and small

You lift my heart,
if only with a smile.
Thank you for being
an angel to me.

I am blessed many times over
And it's all because of you!

Thank you for the cherished memories.

Thank you for the sweet moments.

Thank you for the guidance, my angel.

Glory are the days we spend
In the peace and bounty of a friend.

CATNIP ♥ CURRY ♥ FENNEL ♥ DILL ♥ THYME
MYRTLE ♥ CORIANDER ♥ GARLIC ♥ PARSLEY ♥ GINGER
BASIL ♥ THYME ♥ SAGE ♥ SAVORY ♥ ROSEMARY
CHIVES
BAY ♥ MINT ♥ SAGE
SAVORY

There's
no Love as
sweet as a
child's Love

It's the simple
blessings
that lead our
hearts
to the angels of
love.

As we ponder our
tomorrows
In the precious moments
of today,
Know this my sweet
angel,
I am more thankful than
I can say.

Thank you for being the secret blessing in my life.

When time is the element
you invest,
In both family and
friends, the rewards
are many
And come in the form
of a blessing.

Your gentle heart
Guided me
When I needed it
most.
You are my angel.

Remember, if you are
feeling low,
I am the angel on your
shoulder.

When I close my eyes at the
day's end, It's with the
cherubs the night I spend.
And in the early moments of
dawn's recall, It's you the
angel, I remember
most of all.

Seasons change and bring
with them new opportunities.
Thank you, my guardian
angel,
For staying with me through
changes, big and small.

Through our prayers, we seek guidance.
Through our blessings, wishes are granted.

Your kind words
Reached my heart
When my head
Stopped listening.

Through spirit,
We are able to
witness
The many blessings in
life.

Friend, whenever I think of you I smile.

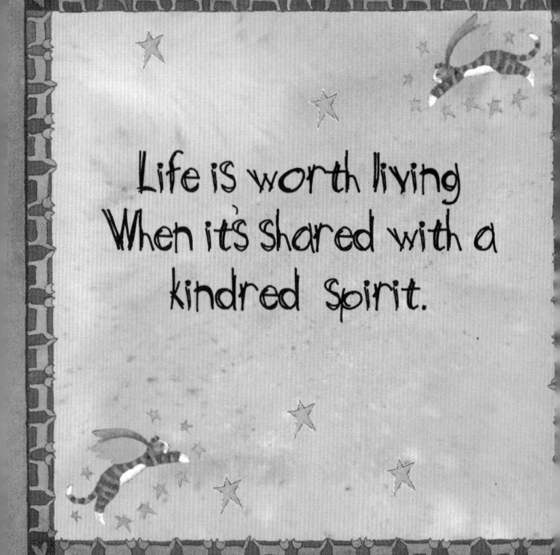
Life is worth living
When it's shared with a
kindred Spirit.

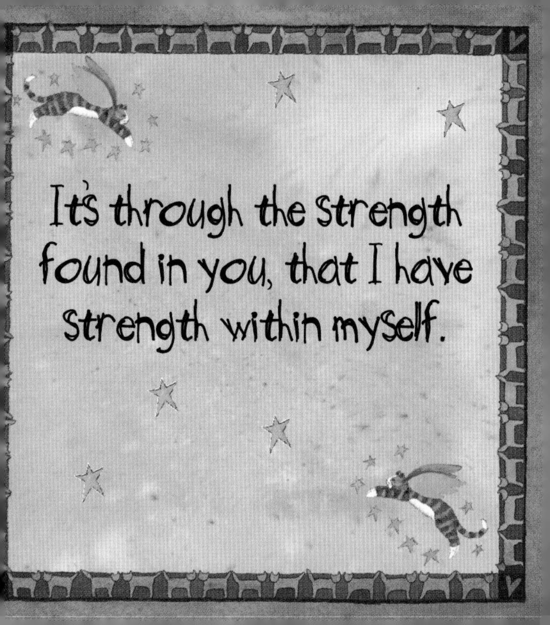
It's through the strength
found in you, that I have
strength within myself.

When we carry burdens
upon narrow shoulders,
The world feels lonely.
Because of you,
My life shines brightly
once again

We all need a guardian
angel to watch over us -
and I need you!

How lucky am I to have
you as my guardian
angel.

I say a blessing
every day for having
you in my life.

With you as my
guardian angel, I am
bound to succeed!

Quiet moments with a
friend are the fondest
memories of the soul.

For times when I was weak,
It is your strength that carried me.

My burdens are few
and my joys are
plenty with you as my
friend.

Angel, you allow my
Spirit the freedom to
reach my dreams.

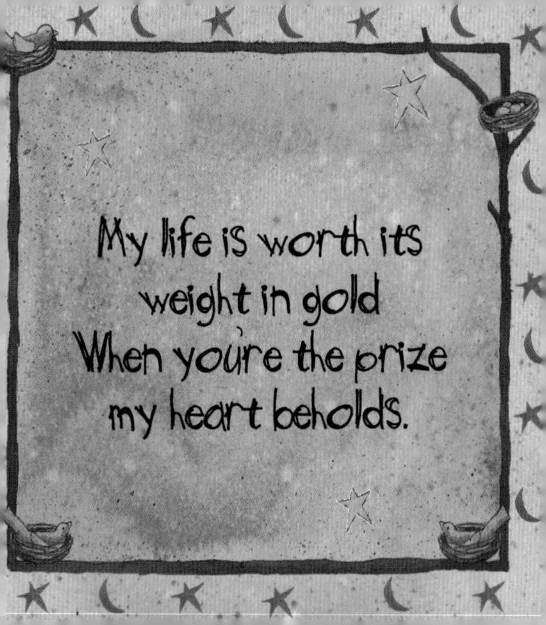
My life is worth its
weight in gold
When you're the prize
my heart beholds.

When I think of
Someone kind, I think
of you my angel.

When I needed help,
you were the angel
that lent me a hand.

Kittens of mine, how I love thee
won't you come
MEOW
CAT NIP

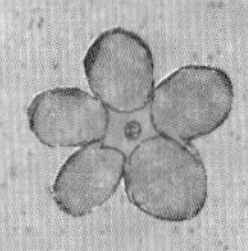

When I was lost, you were the angel that showed me the way.

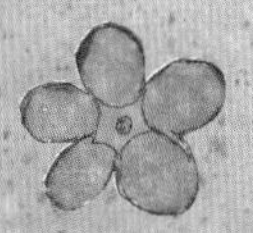

An angel's love
Can fill a heart
As full as a wave
Covers the shore.

Angel, you ease my pain as if it were light as a feather.

Angels come in many forms,
Teachers, doctors, helpers, all.
Have you looked in the mirror lately,
Angel?

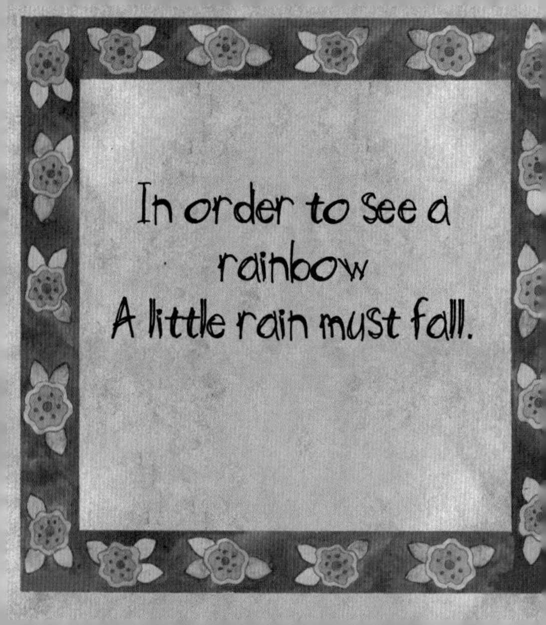
In order to see a
rainbow
A little rain must fall.

Time is never wasted
when it is spent with a
friend.

We know peace
When it lies within us.
We know love
When we share it with a
friend.

You must be the Angel
of Encouragement.

Just the sound of
your laughter brings
happiness to my
face!

With so many
obligations,
And so little time,
I am greatful that our
friendship
Remains our top
priority.

Peace

Life's challenges are really opportunities in disguise!

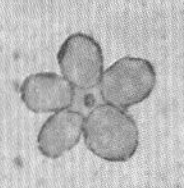

You are the angel
that taught me to
be gentle with
myself.

What do I see when I
look at you?
I see my own happiness
smiling back at me.

You've touched my life
like the rainbow
touches the sky.

Through Spirit,
We are able to witness
The many blessings in
our life.

Your kindness has given me Peace, love and serenity.

Life has a way of
opening us up to
wonderful
blessings.

Upon the day
When I found you
An angel sent
A blessing to me.

You are many things to me.
Above all you are my friend.

When I found trouble,
You guided me.
When I found sadness,
You lifted me.

You have helped me
become
The best me
I can be!

You may count your blessings
By all the little angels
in your life.

Share your love everyday, cuz
love isn't love until you give it away

When I reflect upon my
blessings,
I rejoice in the friend I
found in you.

We are spirits that are connected by a golden thread called love.